Read what people are saying about Janet Perry and *Needlepoint Trade Secrets*:

"Overflowing with tips on every aspect of stitching, Janet M. Perry's *Needlepoint Trade Secrets* deserves a slot in your stitching library. Actually, at its new size, this fun and funny reference tool merits space in your stitcing *bag*! I wouldn't be without my copy. There' s inspiration on every page." **Michelle Hufford, Come to the Point! San Rafael, CA** (shopowner)

"I have Janet Perry's Book - "Needlepoint Trade Secrets" and I think it should be in everyone's library. I keep reading and re-reading this wonderful book that's full of information. . . . I learn something new each time I read it." **Ruth, Las Vegas, NV** (stitcher)

"For five years her dedicated research and wonderful contributions to [About.com] not only have introduced people to needlepoint, but also inspired and informed so many of use in our lifetime's passion for all thing needlepoint." **Rosalyn Cherry-Soliel on her site Stitchamaze.com** (http://www.stitchamaze.com)

". . . indispensible needlepoint newsletter for stitchers of all levels. Whatever you need, Janet will hook you up." **Needlepoint Heaven Links List** (http://www.needlepointheaven.com)

D1402338

NEEDLEPOINT TRADE SECRETS

Second Edition

by Janet M. Perry

ISBN: 1-4196-6533-2 (trade paperback)

Library of Congress Catalog Number
LCCN: 2007904036

Published in 2007 by Napa Needlepoint,
Napa, CA

Printed in the United States of America

For more information about Napa Needlepoint &
Janet M. Perry's stitch guides, books, projects, or
to have her teach, please visit her website at:
http://www.napaneedlepoint.com

This book is dedicated to stitchers everywhere, who have taught me so much.

INTRODUCTION

Needlepoint has been done for centuries, and even though I've been stitching for over 30 years, I still discover new ways to make my stitching better, learn a new stitch, or rediscover something from times past.

This little book shares with you those tips, secrets, and tricks I have learned and which have been taught to me by my teachers, friends, and students.

Enjoy and Keep Stitching!

Janet

TABLE OF CONTENTS

CANVAS

Needlepoint canvas comes in three different types: mono, interlock, and Penelope. Within these types, canvas comes in different mesh sizes (number of holes per inch), colors, and quality. There are also specialized types of canvas for tasks such as making rugs, stitching on fabric, or making clothing.

Mono canvas is most popularly used for hand-painted needlepoint. It has an over-under weave (called a Tabby Weave). Interlock canvas has one set of threads split so that the intersections are locked in place. It is most commonly found in kits. Penelope canvas, also called Duo canvas, has two threads. These threads can be split apart and stitched over singly. Therefore, Penelope canvas is often listed with two numbers, for example 10/20. It is most often found in European canvases.

If an interlock canvas gets out of shape it can be hard to block it back into shape.

Even if you don't know much about the canvas you are using, you can tell something about the quality. Good quality canvas isn't hairy (a sign of short fibers which will be rough on threads), stiff (too much sizing and hard on fibers) or limp (too little sizing and hard to stitch). Untwist the end of a thread of canvas, there will be four or five strands making up the canvas thread.

Canvas is sized according to the numbers of "holes per inch," or HPI. The higher the number the smaller the holes on the canvas. Canvas with 24 HPI is referred to as "Congress Cloth." HPIs higher than 24 are only found on silk gauze, a type of interlock canvas found in HPIs up to 60. You will also find canvas sizes referred to as "mesh." This too refers to the number of holes per inch of canvas.

Canvas while it is generally the same mesh size throughout, can sometimes be off by a thread or so. Needlepoint designers generally take this into account in painting. If you are making your own design and an exact size is important (it usually isn't), count the threads you need, then measure and adjust accordingly.

In general, don't worry about grain on a hand-painted canvas. Designers paint so that the selvage would be on the left or right of the design, even if the piece of canvas is from the middle of the roll.

If the selvage is missing from your canvas, bend the canvas both top to bottom and left to right. Top to bottom is the direction which bends easier. If you do have a selvage edge on your canvas, you don't need to cut it off before stitching, just don't stitch any closer than three threads away from the edge. This is because the holes get smaller as the edges of the canvas are reached.

When you buy or cut canvas, it should always be along a row of holes. Because cutting canvas is hard on scissors, have a special pair for this. I have a pair of Gingher garden shears I use only for this.

Sizing, the thing which makes needlepoint canvas stiff, is also what makes it hard on threads. The rough edges of the sizing scrapes the thread as it passes through the canvas. The lower quality the canvas, the more sizing in it and the harder it will be on threads.

The quality of canvas makes a difference in your work. High-quality canvas is easier on threads, it blocks properly, and it can be manipulated to make different stitches. Most stitchers prefer Zweigart canvas, which always has an orange line in the selvage. If you don't have a selvage, cut a small piece of canvas and note the size. Soak it in warm water for a few minutes. If it shrinks, the canvas is poor quality.

You can do needlepoint on metal or fiberglass screening. Because the holes are rectangular, the designs look a bit different. But it's a great effect.

You can save space and let the canvas relax by taking pieces you aren't stitching off stretcher bars and rolling them up.

As it gets old, canvas loses its sizing and becomes soft. One way to make the canvas stiff again is to put it onto stretcher bars. If you have some old canvas which is unstitched but has lost its sizing, you can also use starch to make it stiffen again (use ONLY on unstitched canvas). But if you need it soft now, scrunch it in your hands for a bit, that breaks up the sizing and softens the canvas.

Are you thinking of using the canvas with metallic threads woven in it? The metallic threads are woven into only one direction. So decide whether these will be vertical or horizontal when you stitch. It's a subtle but important difference: the direction of the canvas can reinforce the design or fight with it.

You may have heard stitchers talking about stitching "with the grain" and wondered why this is important. Not only will it keep your stitching from getting ridges, stitching with the grain will help set the stitches better, making the stitching look more uniform and even.

How can you find the grain? If there is a selvage, it should be on either the right or left side. If there is no selvage, unravel part of one horizontal and one vertical thread; the one which is more wavy is the vertical thread.

Canvas does have a front and back. To find it, hold the canvas up to the light; the side with slightly larger holes is the front.

COLOR

Color is a wonderful mix of scientific fact, theory, and aesthetics. In the study of color, you can approach it from almost any aspect and learn interesting things. A study of color and the practical application of this study can keep you happy for years.

There are some specialized terms for color which will help you understand what you read. **Hue** *is the proper term for the "color." Red, for example, is a hue.* **Value** *is the term used for how light or dark a hue is. White has the highest value and black the lowest.* **Shades** *are a combination of a hue plus black.* **Tints** *are a hue plus white.* **Tones** *are a hue plus gray or the color's complement. Finally, the term* **saturation,** *or* **intensity,** *describes how much of a hue is in the color. If gray, white, black, or the complement are added to a color, it becomes less intense or saturated.*

Want to learn the basics about color? Get a good color wheel and explore.

You can dye your own wool threads with Kool-aid™ and other unsweetened powder drink mixes. Instructions and color cards can be found on the Internet. Because Kool-aid™ is nontoxic, it is a great project to do with kids.

Thread, unlike paint, comes in discrete colors. This means that you have a limited amount of colors you can make based on the colors available in the thread. You can increase this number by using a stranded thread, but the colors are still limited, you can't "mix" an infinite number of colors, as you can with paint.

Many color schemes have one color which is predominant, called the dominant hue. This color brings together a group of colors by being a unifying element. Think of a night sky when there are several dark true blues, perhaps a greenish blue and deep blue-violet. All these colors are unified by dark blue.

If your color scheme is complementary, one color of the pair should dominate.

To check if the colors you have chosen work well together, lay them out in a line. Do any stick out? You might want to find a different color.

Trying out different color schemes before stitching can be a good idea. Draw the outlines of the shapes on canvas and make several copies. Color them in the different color schemes. Take the one you like best to the shop when buying threads.

If your needlepoint seems dull, it might need some contrast in value. Add some darker or lighter threads.

Stumped for a color scheme? Look to those new paint chips which have several coordinating colors on them. Find threads to match the colors and you have your color scheme.

View color combinations in low light to check out the values. Strive for contrast in values in your work.

Color is everywhere, just look. Take a walk, visit a shop, look at a book or magazine. You can find ideas anyplace.

14

White needlepoint canvas makes colors look brighter than when they have a background color stitched. Keep this in mind when choosing colors for your needlepoint.

Preview your color choices by wrapping thread around a strip of cardboard in the approximate proportions you will be using.

If you are a Macintosh user and use OS X, check out Color Burn from Firewheel Designs (http://www.firewheeldesign.com). This little Widget for your Dashboard provides a color scheme of the day, every day.

Want to check the values of your colors? Make a black and white photocopy.

Two colors, of almost equal intensity, where one is cool and the other hot, create a feeling of vibration. This is most effective when the colors are not complementary.

If you want your needlepoint to look sophisticated, use tones – colors blended with gray or the color's complement.

Want your needlepoint to have a warm and cozy feel? Use wools (fuzzy texture) and shades of red and warm browns.

Is the thread color warm or cool? Put it next to another thread and see if it looks redder (warmer) or bluer (cooler) than the other.

If you want a contemporary look to your needlepoint, choose white, black, and pure colors.

Vary a monochromatic color scheme by having several textures -- get this by using different threads or stitches.

Color schemes are typical of periods. Think of how avocado green and brown scream 1970's. Pick a color scheme from a different era to vary a design.

Want a springtime color combination? Include yellow-green — the color of new leaves.

Watery muted pastels, which look like old fabric, can give needlepoint a vintagey look.

Putting a tiny bit of a color's complement next to it will make the color look brighter.

Make an interesting background by finding all your threads of the same color, dividing the background into blocks and using the thread collection to stitch it.

Making a blended needle with one or more strands of a color's complement will dull the color, moving it towards neutral tones.

Japanese design associates particular colors and color schemes with particular seasons. If you want to design a seasonal needlepoint without the usual color combinations, look for information about these. A good book which shows this is *Kimono* by Linda Darby.

Some decorating magazines publish color forecasts (you can also find these on the Internet). Use these to give you fresh ideas for color combinations. Fashion magazines, especially those aimed at teenagers, are also good sources of ideas.

FINISHING

Lovely finishing can make a piece of needlepoint look even better. Many stitchers, myself included, hesitate to have their needlepoint finished. An expensive choice is to have your needlepoint professionally finished. Happily for us, there are many products which you can use to finish needlepoint yourself, with fantastic results. It's also possible to use other items you might find to make fantastic needlepoint. Come with me while we explore the possibilities for finishing.

Keep your mats and backgrounds simple — it's the needlepoint people care about.

If needlepoint will replace fabric upholstery, use the fabric as a guide for the size and shape of the finished stitching.

Making needlepoint "clothing" as ornaments? As a great trick, use small hangers as the ornament hangers. The Studio, a designer and shop in Kansas City, carries them.

Looking for an unusual frame for needlepoint? Try using a small wooden tray, or have an unusual mat (suede?) cut in the outline of your piece.

If you tape the edges of your needlepoint, block after you have removed the tape. Most tapes become loose when wet and won't hold the piece firmly during blocking.

Do you live in a humid area? Never use steel nails to block your needlepoint.

A tip from old books: Needlepoint which has been blocked or which isn't badly out of shape can be "freshened" with a steam iron. Put the needlepoint face down on some towels. Hold the iron, set for steam, about 1/4 inch above the needlepoint. I don't know, but this might also work with personal steamers for clothes as well.

Make a tray from a frame. Add drawer handles to the short edges and little feet to the bottom.

If you are framing your needlepoint under glass, ask for spacers to be added to keep the glass from touching the needlepoint.

There are non-glare acrylics out now for framing which are considerably lighter than glass, and, sometimes, UV protective too!

If you are fitting needlepoint into a rimmed box top, don't stitch to the edge, use Fray Check™ or white glue to stabilize your cut edge.

Test and pick your framing material when the needlepoint is almost, but not quite, finished. Then you know what you want and the shop can order it. The materials will be in about the time the needlepoint is done.

I am always looking for ways to finish things inexpensively. Recently I bought a watch in a "picture frame" box. The opening is 2.5" square. I have a little piece of needlepoint which is just that size. Now the box is not a pretty color, so I am going to decoupage some textured paper on it to cover up the weird plastic. But when it's done, it will be cute and the box didn't cost a dime!

Want to cut costs on your framing? Have the **outside** dimensions of your mat cut to fit a standard size frame, then buy a ready-made frame instead of having a custom frame made. Many frame shops carry these frames and may even do the work for you (at a fee).

If you are finishing your needlepoint as a stand-up, think about adding a small sachet inside.

Large (size 100) button forms work beautifully with Congress Cloth to make Christmas ornaments. If the background of your ornament is open, cover the form with cloth first for a more finished look.

Susan learned this great tip at a class: "Be brave when cutting the canvas after all the hours of stitching. After blocking, just run a thin line of white glue (Elmer's) around the entire edge of the canvas where you want to cut the designed piece. It doesn't take much glue to secure all the yarns. After glue is dry, bravely cut on the outside of the glue, making your piece the perfect size. I remember the first try. I was so scared that everything was going to unravel and fall apart!!"

Make an international tree with ornaments of flags, needlepointed and then finished as small boxes with ribbon trim on top.

Are you making something which is going to go in one of those metal rounds like those used on the porcelain boxes? I've always had problems with getting them to fit nicely into the tops because needlepoint is often too thick for the fitting. Here's a way to avoid the problem.

First don't stitch all the way to the edge of the circle you have drawn, leave about a 1/4 inch border of unstitched canvas. This will be covered by the rim of the top so it won't show. Then you can use glue or Fray Check™ to stabilize the edges after you cut them out. Voila! The needlepoint fits nicely.

Easels of any size can be an alternative for displaying framed needlepoint.

Use strips of canvas, finish them like a pillow and fill them with weights of your choice to make a holder to keep books open.

Ornaments don't have to be just for Christmas. Use feather or open trees as places to display seasonal canvases finished as ornaments.

You can use stretcher bars to stretch your canvas as well! I had to stretch an ornament for my mom yesterday and since it's small I didn't want to get out my huge stretching frame. So I used stretcher bars. Here's how to do it. Wet the piece to be stretched. Put the frame over something with a grid. Tack down one corner. Stretch the canvas so the finished needlepoint is square and tack the diagonally opposite corner. Repeat the process for the other two corners. Now do the center of opposite sides, still making sure the finished needlepoint is square to the grid. Then add tacks as necessary to keep all the sides straight. Put it someplace flat to dry. The height of the bars will allow air circulation.

Sometimes you want to be able to change the look of something like a needlepoint pincushion or a boxtop. There is a way to do this before you finish it. First off, don't glue anything in place, especially the padding covered with needlepoint. Second, using narrow satin or grosgrain ribbon, make a little tab, which you glue to the undersides of the covered piece. For large pieces, do one for each side, for smaller pieces, just one is enough. Then place the covered piece into its frame. You can use the tabs to pull it out and replace it.

If you want an option to display your ornament-sized stand-up all year long, add a button to the back to secure the hanger.

If your finishing item has a plastic cover, use it to protect lightly stitched items.

If your piece has long diagonal stitches, keep them from snagging and getting loose by keeping the work on the frame until it goes to the finisher.

Want a quick way to make a needlepoint belt? Buy some grosgrain ribbon the width of your finished needlepoint and some "D" rings. Use the ribbon to back the finished needlepoint and loop one end through the rings. Voila! A belt.

There are lots of other uses for all those belt canvases. Try them as basket bands, purse straps, suspenders, shoe straps, camera straps, or hat bands.

Brenda Hart, a fantastic needlepoint stitcher, makes long canvases, slightly wider than belts and has them finished with hooks on the ends. Then she uses them as interchangeable purse straps.

INSPIRATION

What inspires your needlepoint? Is it a picture in a book? A photograph? A combination of colors? A great canvas? Artists (and we're artists) see inspiration all around them. You can too. This section has lots of ideas for finding sources of inspiration and for using those sources to create needlepoint.

Keep a notebook with your stitching to record ideas for how to stitch canvases from your stash and what you stitched on a canvas.

Your china can be great inspiration for needlepoint. Use the pattern to pick colors and then design a geometric or corner plaid design from them.

Have a bulletin board near your desk? Use it to put up inspiring pictures of needlepoint or photos/pictures you want to stitch.

Keeping a notebook of pictures you like can help inspire you to do beautiful needlepoint you design yourself.

Dover publishes a wonderful series of pattern design books which are copyright free–great inspirations for needlepoint.

Do you see pictures of things you like in magazines or books? I am on a major reorganizing binge this summer, so I'm trying to put stuff in order. I have boxes and boxes of magazines to go through. When I find a picture I like in a magazine, I dog-ear the page. Then when I'm going through it again I tear out the page and put it into a box. Cutting and pasting into my notebooks will be a fall task.

For books, I use Post-it Note flags. If I find a drawing or picture I want to use as inspiration or adapt, on goes a flag. I used to dog-ear pages (much to my DH's chagrin) but some of my books are a mess because of that. This is neater and the tags are easy to find later.

I keep a small dish with Post-it flags on my desk and grab a pad to use when I'm looking at a book.

I love the designs on wrapping paper; they usually have a limited number of colors, which makes them great color schemes for needlepoint.

Hooked rug patterns (the line drawings) and coloring books can be a great resource for needlepoint designs.

After awhile I get burned out with stitching. Does this happen to you? When it does do one of two things – look at books of needlepoint to get inspired or work on one of those mindless projects where you can just stitch and not think. Rent a good movie, listen to music and just relax.

Your library probably has a large arts and crafts section; go and browse sometimes, looking for books on different periods, countries or types of crafts.

Did you see a color scheme you liked in a magazine, or a picture. Tear it out, or use a color card to match the colors and list them on a card.

It works great when you see a listing of "hot" colors in a magazine, or sample paint chip schemes in the paint store.

Sometimes you need to think about a canvas and the stitches and threads you want to use. The best way to do this is find a place where you will see it often and hang it up. I've got mine taped (using that white tape for canvas) onto a shelf in my office. On the shelf I've put the threads I have already selected for the canvas. There it will sit as I think about the way I want to approach the canvas. This is a great way to let ideas percolate and to give you inspiration.

If your house is overrun with magazines, tear out the pages you want to save immediately and save them in a box or folder to add to your notebooks later.

Speaking of paint chips, those paint chip schemes usually list a main color, a secondary color, and one or two accents. Here you have a ready-made needlepoint color scheme. Use the dominant color for the background, the secondary color for a main color in the foreground or focal point. and the accents for accents in the focal point or as small accents in the background.

Sometimes the best way to learn about color and texture is to work with it. A while ago I bought a Seka & Co. cross stitch graph of a crazy quilt. Since I can never leave well enough alone, I decided to do the piece in needlepoint, instead of cross stitch, with just pink and red threads instead of multiple colors, and on 18-mesh canvas instead of 14-count Aida. My plan was to see how different threads (23 in all) work, and to thereby create a "red" sampler.

For each patch in the design, except for the gold ones, I used a different red or pink thread from my stash. To give me a wide selection, I pulled every pink or red thread I could find, so there were many. I did a patch at a time. Once one patch was done, I looked for the next thread.

The whole process was great, didn't take that long, and the finished result is quite excellent. In fact it was so much fun, I'm thinking about doing several other color studies of this kind, using different colors.

Whenever I can, I look at home decor magazines; they always have so many interesting patterns.

LEARNING

No matter how long you have been stitching, there's plenty more to learn about needlepoint. Visit sites on the Web, join a guild chapter, take a class at your local shop. Every needlepoint piece you stitch will teach you something – a new stitch, a new thread, a cool way to make letters. Look at books, even old ones for new ideas. Look at your friends' needlepoint. You may not like the design, but that background stitch may be perfect in another color for a piece in your stash.

Do you want to learn more about needle-point? Explore the website from the American Needlepoint Guild (http://www.needlepoint.org). There's tons of great information there.

Wish you had a needlepoint guild near you? Why not think about starting an informal stitching group meeting weekly or monthly? This can be the start of a guild.

If you are having trouble understanding directions, try reading them out loud.

Needlepoint books from the '70s have lots of great information, if you can get past the color combinations. Library book sales can often be wonderful places to get them. Some sales sell by the inch, some by the book – but always at prices far below what you would pay at a used book store. This comes to mind because I was at one of the local sales yesterday and came away with about six great needlepoint books for $5. These included *Needlepoint from Great American Quilt Designs* in hardcover (I have the paperback already), *Sculpted Needlepoint Design* and *Needlepoint Letters and Numbers.*

If you love books or if you love needlepoint books, these sales are really worth checking out.

If you are having trouble understanding how a stitch is made, try drawing it, just as you would stitch it, on graph paper.

Using a graph? Try putting a needle, pencil, or chopstick pointing to the line you are following.

Do you have a problem like arthritis or fibromyalgia which keeps you from stitching sometimes? When this happens to me, I get out some of my project or design books and look for ideas for future projects.

If you are just learning needlepoint, think both big and small. Look for projects on **bigger** mesh sizes and look for projects which are **smaller** in size. As you gain experience, use smaller mesh sizes and bigger projects.

It's a wonderful learning experience to work on a challenging piece. It's a fantastic experience conquering something difficult.

Is that background stitch not coming out even? This happened to me last week. I pulled out sections of this background four times. That's when I realized that as much as I liked the stitch, the combination wasn't working, so I ripped it out again and used a simpler stitch. But I sure know what to look for the next time I use it.

Sometimes making regular time to stitch with a friend or two is a wonderful way to learn.

Often shops have times for drop-in stitching. They are a time for people to get together and visit and stitch. They are great learning opportunities as well, because you can learn and get ideas.

Want to learn from a well-known teacher, but can't travel to a class or seminar? Check out the teacher's site on the Web. Many of them offer online classes, popularly called Cyberclasses.

Check out your library for older stitch books, including ones for techniques like filet crochet, knitting stitch patterns, or embroidery. These are great sources of new stitch ideas and patterns. Some of my favorite ideas have come from knitting books.

Don't live near a guild chapter? Look at the online chapters for the popular guilds.

MATERIALS

You might think that needlepoint is simply a matter of thread, canvas, and a needle. But there are so many things out there which make wonderful tools for needlepoint. So many of these things can make your needlepoint look better, or help you stitch more easily. Common materials can be used in creative ways for needlepoint; needlepoint materials can be used in ways to make your stitching easier. Adopting some of these tips can make your stitching look more beautiful.

What are "usual stitching supplies?" These are the things you need in order to stitch comfortably. They should always include needles, something to cut the thread, and something to hold (ends of threads (even if it's a paper cup). If you are going to a class they should also include stretcher bars and tacks, if you haven't done this at home already. Depending on your habits, the usual supplies could include a lamp, a stand, magnifiers, or reading glasses.

A thoughtful gift for a stitcher is a gift certificate to a local needlework shop.

If you use a needle which is too large for the canvas, your motion will be jerky and your tension will suffer. If you use a needle which is too small, it will be difficult to thread.

Secretary's correction fluid, like Wite-out™ or Liquid Paper™ can be used to cover marks on white canvas in a pinch.

Cut the tails of threads off immediately after you secure them. This prevents them from getting caught in future stitching.

Mark the center of your scroll rods and stretcher bars with permanent marker.

With tapestry needles, the higher the number, the smaller the needle.

Speaking of magnets, get one of those extendable magnets and keep it near your sewing chair. Use it from time to time to sweep the area for needles.

I am now making sure I have a magnet on every canvas for holding my needles. All well and good, but I carry the canvases around everywhere, and I'm always losing needles. Now I put the needle onto the magnet inside the stretcher bars (the back of the canvas). They get jostled much less this way.

Do you like to use 4H pencils for drawing needlepoint designs? Better stationery stores will have 4H lead for mechanical pencils. Buy a pencil and use this lead in it (keep it away from everything else) and you have it right at hand.

Do you need a sharp-pointed needle for a needlepoint technique? Use crewel or chenille needles. They have sharper points but big eyes (like Tapestry needles). They are sized the same way as Tapestry needles.

When stitching a kit, always buy at least one package of needles the same size as enclosed in the kit. You always lose needles and it's good to have extras on hand.

I inadvertently found a good use for those stitcher's magnets which have lost their backs. One of mine fell between the cushion and the frame of my stitching chair. I found it when a needle fell as well. But, happily, the needles which had fallen (there were three) had stuck to the magnet.

Try a natural daylight bulb (available in fluorescent and incandescent) in your stitching lamp.

If you like to work in hand, buy some French clothes clips. These vinyl-coated spring clips come in bright colors and are great for holding rolled canvas.

Looking for a great flat needlecase? Transform a cigarette case or business card case with glued in magnets and you've got something distinctive and flat.

A tip for using fabric markers: If they seem to be drying out, cap them and keep them point down for a while so the ink can run back towards the tip.

A little, almost flat, Japanese sauce dish works great to hold beads.

Look for Victorian hair receptacles as a place to store orts. Find them in antique stores. Pretty jars without lids also work well.

A metal mint box works great as a place to store needles.

Try your hardware store for stitching supplies. Look for wire brushes, cheap sturdy thumbtacks, and lots more.

I took one look at a bead embroidery book and I was entranced. Now I want to go buy beads and play. But I HATE sharp needles – the stock-in-trade for beading. John James makes ballpoint beading needles. They are short and have dull points like Tapestry needles. Combine these with a thread like Silk Bella from Kreinik and you can bead away!

Use a small pillow filled with buckwheat hulls as a frame weight.

As you stitch, needles can get bent or their holes can get compressed. Throw these out.

If you like smaller needles, check out a quilt shop. Sometimes you can buy needles in 25 packs. Put them in your needlecase.

Don't ever store needles stitched through an area of the canvas that is going to be stitched. They can discolor or distort the fabric. Store needles on magnets, in needle holders, or in the margins of the canvas.

Corroded needles can discolor yarn. Throw any needles with rust or dark spots away.

Curved needles can be used when you can't get to the back of the work. Since these are usually sharp, use a file to dull the point.

You can rubber band all the similar size stretcher bars together. That way it's easy to see if you need to buy some. So you know the size of random stretcher bars, use permanent pens to mark the size at each end, place your initials in the center of each side.

If you use the same scissors for all threads, cut metallics near the hinge.

To make it easier to lift tacks or staples, use a lever staple remover and put it under the canvas and on top of the stretcher bars.

If you use pink hair tape to park your thread, roll it up like a pin curl before taping.

From Peter at The Red Thread: Do you want to make those button covered stitcher's magnets? Scotch brand Super Glue keeps the buttons on the best.

Don't use masking tape to cover the edge of canvases. It does bad things. The adhesive wears out, flakes off, and it stains the edges of the canvas. The same thing applies to drafting tape.

From Peter at The Red Thread: Think about covering a stitcher's magnet with seed beads. To do this, take Ceramicoat glaze, brush it on the magnet, then stick it in some seed beads.

Take the time to use artist's tape to cover the edges of your canvas. Find an art supply store which carries it. It is stiffer than masking tape and has a different kind of adhesive. The adhesive is not as sticky as masking tape, so you need to press it to the canvas. But it holds like crazy and doesn't stain. It is "that white tape" used by needlepoint shops.

Need a way to brush your needlepoint but don't have a Bunko Brush (wire brush) around? A new hard bristle toothbrush or the hook side of a piece of VELCRO® both work wonders to raise pile.

Make yourself a kit to store your tools by using a decorative tin; mine's from France and had caramels in it originally.

Keep your empty spools and cards from threads. I keep mine in a basket and use them to wind threads. I first heard this tip at a local shop, where one customer put **every** thread she bought on empty Kreinik spools.

From needlepoint designer Ro Pace, who posted information about a wonderful tool on the ANG list, a reducing glass: You can find these in quilt shops. Quilters often use them to check the balance of colors and pattern in a quilt. You can do the same in your needlepoint. Using the reducing glass can help you find colors which "stick out" before the piece is finished, so you can make your needlepoint look better than ever. I'm planning on asking for one for Christmas.

When you remove stitching, do you find leftover "fuzz" or stray strands from the cut threads? Buy a make-up "spoolie" or mascara brush. They look like mascara wands but don't have the make-up with them. Pull them through the holes of canvas to catch the strays.

ORGANIZATION

*If you look at a bookstore's shelves, organization seems to be a constant problem. If you looked at my desk, my stitching chair, or my studio, you would know that it's true. But being organized means having things where **YOU** can find them and having your stitching things put together so that stitching is a pleasure. For you that might be putting all the supplies for a project together in an envelope or pouch. For me that might be zipper bags safety pinned to the canvas.*

These are some of my favorite tips. Even though many of them are small things, they make a HUGE difference in your stitching life. Think about it: How many times have you bought the same thread because you can't find the skeins you already own? When was the last time you couldn't find a needle? Being organized is not about being compulsive; it's about making your life work for you so that you have more time to stitch and can take more pleasure in it.

You should store canvas rolled up instead of folded. Use mailing tubes, wine bottle cases, or even a small, new wastepaper basket to keep it rolled. Smaller canvases should be stored flat.

Do you have lots of little threads to store? I am trying to keep my threads for temari separate from my needlepoint threads. And, of course, they are overflowing the box. So I have taken out my grandmother's lovely sewing cabinet (you know, the kind which opens out). You can still find pieces like this for tables or floors at craft and sewing stores and at places like Hold Everything. They make outstanding places to store your materials as well as attractive pieces of furniture.

From a reader: You can use inexpensive wine storage racks to store stretcher bars or canvas.

Have you seen those colored plastic envelopes at the office supply store? Think of using them as stylish, portable project holders. They won't come apart like plastic bags will.

From a reader: Use skirt hangers; hang the canvas on the hanger and then put the threads in a bag hung around the hanger.

Make a thread holder for your stand by using an old-fashioned wide-toothed plastic hair comb. Your threads can rest between the teeth.

Make your file cabinet pretty. Use file folders with patterns on them to organize your records and notes.

CD cabinets make great places to store your fibers.

Make your own color card with a piece of thin cardboard and 1" lengths of each color. Be sure to mark down thread name and color number.

Finding a place for orts during classes can be a real problem. One lady in my class suggested using an empty boutique-size tissue box. They are easy to find, disposable and cheap. I thought this was a great idea.

It's a good idea to take time at least once a year to clean up your stash. I am taking advantage of my kids' being home this week to do my annual cleaning. Of course a contributing factor is that I couldn't find anything at all.

So today, I went through the drawers of projects and the shelves in my closet. I group like things together so I can find them. This means all needlepoint canvas, all cross stitching fabric, items for finishing, fabrics for finishing, trims, stitched canvases, unstitched canvases, projects with threads, empty project bags, and so on.

Whenever I do this, I always find canvases I won't stitch and those will be going in our guild's auction. I also found a project I swapped for another project with a friend and never gave to her. And the benefit is, you can actually get to the clothes in the closet.

Looking cheap picture frames? Try your local thrift store. My community has one which is local and all the money stays in the community. While I don't always find things, I do find them often enough to make it worthwhile.

Keep skeined threads on big rings (like notebook rings) to see all the colors at once.

I have now become a convert to nice bags for holding my WIP's (Works in Progress); no more plastic bags for me! Many companies make these durable and fashionable heavy bags with zippers across the top. Basics (available at Wal-Mart, Target and other stores) has sets of three bags of various sizes for about $5. Often these are clear, so you can see what's inside. Many companies are also making larger bags, some even big enough to hold your frame. I also have some wonderful bags sewn with tartan ribbons. They look great, are mostly waterproof, and make you feel as if your materials are as special as the finished needlepoint.

Floss-a-way or other small zipper bags can be great for holding threads for a single project. Put your threads in them and put on a ring. Portable and easy to find!

Do you have replacement insurance on your belongings? We do and I had always wondered how to value my threads and such. Happily for me, the Organized Expressions software includes a field for value. You should start including this information in whatever system you use to inventory your thread. So now when I go buy threads, not only do I add them to the inventory, but I also make sure that thread (and every other skein of it in inventory) has a value, taken from the sales slip. This information is crucial in the case of a loss (God forbid) or if you need to put a value on your work for charity.

To give yourself another easy place to keep needles: I have been keeping them on top of a small metal box to store stitching tools. So when you finish a piece, put the needle there instead of trying to find your needlecase, at least for awhile.

Shoe and sweater bags make great open storage for wools and other yarns in large skeins.

A lovely and inexpensive place to store threads is in cigar boxes. If you don't know a cigar smoker, go to your local tobacconists, they almost always have empty cigar boxes and they start at about $1. Look for all-cedar ones, not the ones with cardboard. The cedar is a natural moth repellent. I label mine with a labelmaker to show what type of thread is inside.

What do you do when you have lots of stitching which must be done? I watch TV, usually a movie, although I also like sporting events. What is ideal is something which is interesting but not so compelling that you forget to stitch. Subtitled movies are definitely out (you have to pay too much attention). My family knows when I'm really pressed to get something done, because I will rent two movies a night.

Do you have a car with a pocket in it, like my minivan? Use it as a place to store a permanent "car project."

When you find a project bag you like, stock up.

Awhile ago I bought some small plastic containers with snap-on lids at a Dollar store. They are about the size of an Altoids® box, and were too cute. I now use them for my portable Ort Port. When I'm stitching and not at home, which happens lots lately. I whip it out and open it so that my thread ends go into the box. Then I can dump it out once I get home. Mint tins also work well for this, as long as the top stays shut.

Are you like me and keep the threads for a project in a zipper bag and the project on a frame? Well, I "lost" the threads for one of my seminar projects after I got home because the frame was one place and the threads in another. So now I use a thumbtack from the frame to put the thread bag with the project. It makes things much easier to track.

Do you have more than one project going at once? Buy a large, flat basket which could hold your current projects. Mine, I'm afraid, is almost laundry basket size and full.

Do you ever find yourself bored with the project you are working on? Or are you starting to feel guilty about the pile of UFO's (unfinished objects) which clutter your entire house? Then you might want to consider using a rotation system. There is a fantastic one developed by Chris Nauta, which is popular. I have just started using one and I am really pleased with the results. Mine is a slight adaptation of the standard system. This is what I do:

First, have a basic rotation of five pieces. Pick pieces with different amounts left to do, using different techniques etc. Make sure there are at least two really fast projects on the list so you feel like you are accomplishing something. Then, write them down in order. Work on each one in rotation, for no more than ten hours total before going on to the next one.

After finishing a piece, a new piece gets added to the list. Interspace urgent projects among those on your list.

Need a smaller toolbox for class? Try using a cosmetic bag. Most of the time they zipper shut and they come in a variety of sizes.

Store tapestry needles of the same size in pill bottles, film canisters, or empty, washed spice jars. Be sure to mark the outside with the size.

For pearl cotton in balls, buy the smallest size Rubbermaid® container. Using a heated metal skewer or knitting needle, poke a hole in the top. Thread the end of the thread through the hole and tape the label on the side. This keeps your thread labeled and neat.

Keep a running list of the things you need at the needlework shop.

Buy Floss-a-way bags in packs and bring a set of those to the class. As soon as they get a kit, students put each thread into a bag and label it. During the class they put extra strands, etc., back into the bags. This prevents a tangle in the kit bag (my problem) and they never have to worry about missing labels, since they labeled the bag.

I have been buying WAY TOO MANY canvases at the January sales. I usually have this problem, so it shouldn't be that surprising. Now, I am feeling overwhelmed again. I am trying to finish as much as I can before Easter. I have ranked unfinished projects from least needing to be done to most, and am working down the list, using the rotation system. It's good every now and again to go through your stash and re-rank what needs to be done. If you are like me, there are plenty of surprises there.

Need to do some major organizing? Assign rewards to yourself such as an hour of stitching time for completing each part. Not only is it motivating, taking time to relax will get you refreshed for the next job.

Watching TV is a great time for organization. Find a project to organize while you watch your favorite shows. I pick these times to work on UFO's, and have finished four in two weeks.

There are two extremely large sizes of Ziploc® bags which make great project bags and can even hold fairly large projects.

If you're storing things in bins, boxes, or drawers, put labels on them which are big enough to see and which face out. That way you don't need to remember which box has the finishing supplies.

Keep a record of the threads you use for certain effects. Put them on index cards and buy a small case to hold them. The next time you want that effect, you can use the card instead of relying on your memory.

Keep a sheet with a list of the sizes of stretcher bars you have with your bars. You won't buy sizes you already own.

List your projects to be done and attach it to your computer. As you finish each thing, cross it off.

Evaluate your projects and prioritize them when making a list. Look at due dates and whether you have the materials. If you don't, list the threads you need to get.

Finally, look at how far along you are. The projects which are at the top of all lists get done first. I finished one project this morning and should complete my second this afternoon.

I've decided that all those plastic bags hanging around just are not very pretty, or necessarily good for the threads. So I'm going to be making some changes over the next week. Projects I am currently working on at home are going to have the threads in small baskets (I get them at garage sales and thrift shops). These can then look at least colorful on the table by my stitching chair.

Projects to be done in the future are going to go into one of those frames with the wire basket drawers. Yes, threads will still be in zipper bags, but I'm hoping that I can prioritize and organize better this way (four drawers) and that, being in my closet instead of on the floor, it will look neater.

Does your LNS (Local Needlework Shop) have an electronic version of their newsletter? Think about switching to that. It saves postage, always a good thing, and you can set up a folder on your computer to keep issues.

Set realistic goals for your stitching. Take into account how much time you have to stitch each day.

A great tip from reader Dorothy Hartel: "Everyone has those camera film canisters with the plastic lid (although with digital cameras they may become an antique). For those fibers that are wide like ribbons/tape I stick one end under the lid to stabilize it (or tape it to the side) and then carefully wrap the ribbon part around the canister to reduce the kinks and wrinkles and then again use the lid to hold it. It also works well with those threads that unravel quickly when cut."

If you store needlework or threads in plastic bags, leave them open, and not tightly packed, stored in a cool, dry, dark place. This will keep the fibers from rotting.

Keep the threads for your current project together (and pretty) by using an inexpensive basket near your stitching chair.

I used to have a silk box. In it went all my stranded silks. Recently I couldn't find a silk I knew I had. So, I separated them and put the different brands into drawers.

PHOTOGRAPHING NEEDLEPOINT

The camera on your phone is great for capturing a quick photo of a finished project to share on your blog.

But what if you want to go one step further and make photos of your needlepoint really stand out? Photographing needlepoint to look its best doesn't require deep knowledge of photography, adopting some simple ideas can make those photos look even better.

Try to photograph your pieces on a bright but cloudy day. There won't be a problem with sun reflection. Another possibility is to photo outside under a roof which filters the light but doesn't put things in shadow.

The best backgrounds for photographing needlepoint are neutral colored with little texture.

Don't photograph needlepoint against a rug, it will look dirty.

Frame your photo so the entire piece is displayed.

Are you photographing for print publication? Then the resolution should be at least 300x300 dpi.

If you need to use a flash, make sure there is another source of light on the piece, coming from a different direction. This prevents unpleasant shadows.

You can diffuse the light from your flash by taping a white plastic bag in front of it.

If you aren't using a flash, bounce light off reflective surfaces (like those photographer's umbrellas). Try to go with three light sources. They should all be the same kind of light. One should be behind the needlepoint and aimed at the background; two should be in front of the object and about 45 degrees off center.

The glare of a flashbulb takes detail away from photographs, which is a problem when photographing needlepoint.

Even if your hands are steady (mine aren't) a tripod is good for taking pictures of needlepoint. When buying one look for one with a ball head.

If you need a photo of a piece which is finished but not framed, leave it on the stretcher bars for the photo, then crop the picture to leave out the unstitched part.

From a reader: Take pics with "open flash" focus. Set your lens for flash. Open your lens, trigger flash, immediately close lens.

Need a photo of a finished Christmas ornament and it's not Christmas? Use a pine tree in your yard as a background.

Smaller pieces don't need to be photographed, they can be scanned. Lay them flat against the scanner and go.

Looking at digital cameras? Look for one with at least 3.1 megapixels. This will allow you to get images at 300 dpi.

The background of your photo should contrast with the needlework. If the piece is light, use a dark background, if dark, use a light background.

You can become part of the "social networking" trend almost immediately by setting up a free site with pictures of your needlepoint projects. Flickr (http://www.flickr.com) is one place to do this. Upload, label and go.

Take a look at the websites for your favorite designers or shops, they might have picture galleries for finished work. Let them know you have a picture of a project, they may want to add it.

PLANNING

If you are like me, you think about needlepoint – most of the time. It's not daydreaming, it's planning. I think about the new canvas which came and what stitches to use. I see a new thread and immediately I think about the canvases in my stash. I go to a shop and buy threads for future projects.

But planning needlepoint is so much more than this. It's figuring out what would make the perfect needlepoint for someone as a gift. It's thinking out the project before you begin to stitch so there is the right balance of threads and stitches to showcase the canvas, it's picking a border which will fit.

Planning your needlepoint in advance will make it better, always, no matter what the subject or your level of expertise.

Every canvas should include some Basketweave. It helps define the decorative stitches, and gives the eye a place to rest.

Plan your borders from the center out, to be sure they fit.

Graph only one corner of a border and then rotate it (or the canvas) as you stitch.

Unless you are doing a repeating pattern, figure on leaving at least one inch all around the design for background.

Test-drive a canvas by putting the unstitched canvas in the location where it will live.

Think of your borders as the frame of your piece. It should set off the work.

Does your family have a typical saying or joke? Make that the centerpiece of a small needlepoint piece.

Use a person's hobby as the subject for a needlepoint to make a great gift. My husband loves baseball, so I made a nutcracker ornament of a player from his favorite team and used the colors from his favorite era. I then changed the hair and face to look like his favorite player and added his number. It's completely unique and perfect for him.

I found a very old stitching notebook this week. Here's a tip from it for figuring out if a border will fit. Count the number of holes along the side where the border will be. Divide that number by the stitch count in holes of the stitch you want to use, less 1 (for a 6-hole stitch you would divide by 5). If the number comes out even, the stitch will fit the border.

Pick a subject or designer you like and collect canvases to match.

How many square inches of a color are in that background? There are a couple of ways to figure this out. If there is lots of background, just ignore the foreground and find the area of the finished piece (multiply the two sides together). Then divide that by the area covered by one skein of the thread.

If the piece doesn't have much background or the background is too broken for this to work, cut out a piece of index card or cardboard to one inch square. Place this over and over again onto the canvas in rows, counting as you go. That will tell you about how many square inches are in this color. Divide that number by the number of inches covered by the skein. Round up, or add another skein for insurance.

If you are working several pieces by the same designer, pick out the colors for all at the same time. This keeps the pieces coordinated. Some colors and threads should be the same across all the canvases. Using the same stitch and/or thread for a background is an easy way to coordinate.
But make sure you write it down. Many designers add to their collections. It would be terrible if those new nativity figures didn't match your original set because you forgot the thread you used.

Are you stitching a series of canvases? Pick the threads and then keep them together in a project bag. Even if only a little bit of thread is needed, pick from that group, it will add consistency to the series.

Have you ever felt like a needlepoint you have done looks confused? Too many colors, too many threads, too many stitches? If you are like me, you are probably brimming over with ideas, but having too much variation leads to finished needlepoint which just looks like a hodgepodge. If you stitch from your stash, this can be an even bigger problem. Some of these canvases you may never finish.

The trick here is to control some of the aspects of your design, in order to highlight other ones. Sometimes, the design tells you what to do. Perhaps it has LOTS of colors in it, then keep to only a few different threads and even fewer stitches. Sometimes, you want to show off many stitches. Then pick fewer colors and use only one or two types of threads.

There are many needlepoint pieces which don't follow these guidelines and which work beautifully. But I'm willing to guess that many of the problem pieces in your stash are like mine, they suffer from being overwhelming (and therefore confusing).

PREPARING TO STITCH

Needlepoint is a real pleasure when you don't have to spend time remembering which color is which, unhooking threads snagged by the raw canvas edges, or rooting through your stash looking for a thread. Preparing to stitch may not take much time, but it reaps benefits the entire time you stitch your project.

My grandmother had a saying "More hurry, less speed." She was a seamstress and her tools were always in perfect shape (I still have some of them). Before she began any project, she prepared everything. And the prep time showed. She was a speed demon and everything was perfect. I'm much less meticulous and so I find that often I have to redo sections because I didn't prepare. Or I can't stitch away from home because I forgot an extra needle, or brought the wrong thread. If I spent those few minutes preparing better I wouldn't have these problems.

The holes in bare canvas should never be clogged with knots, sizing or even paint.

Protect your canvas from dirt when not working by covering it. An old pillowcase is perfect.

Tie short lengths of each color of thread in the margins (on the color guide if possible). This will help you remember.

From a reader: Include a piece of paper with your name and address inside every project bag. It can be returned to you if lost.

From my friend Beth: She puts all the threads for a project in a bag with the name of the project on it. She uses those little metal needle threaders and adds a chain of beads through the middle hole with clip or a ring. She then attaches it to the canvas so she always has a threader handy. She keeps each project in its own large storage bag so to keep it clean and organized and carries them in a large bag everywhere she goes. She says: "This is not a big tip just something I find that makes it easier for me so do not run all around. I also keep a small basket on the stand by my couch with extra needles, cutters, threaders, hand cream, and Thread Magic."

Think about lighting conditions when you pack your "take-along" project. If you are working on something dark, take along a light-colored piece just in case.

Do you find the pen skips when marking canvas? Pull the pen towards you. This often makes it easier to draw.

From Helen, a fellow stitcher: "I use a music stand for my needlework items and chart. The stand itself can be made higher or lower and also the three individual legs can be too, so it can fit most places. The ledge, on which I put a magnetic board to attach my chart with either the magnetic strips or a clip (as in closing bags of chips etc.), can be moved forward or back. I can hang my scissors, needle threader, laying tool from any of the jutting parts of the stand. You can hang thread over these or the ledge. I have also made a smaller version of the ort collector/pincushion (which usually hangs over the arm of a chair) and hung that on the stand. I love this gadget, and the best thing is that it's really inexpensive and available at any musical instrument store."

You can use your textile markers or watered down acrylic paint in a color close to the thread's color to cover areas where you will have open stitches so the canvas won't show through. The little specks which appear without coloring (or using colored canvas) are called "needlepoint dandruff." The result doesn't have to be dark, even, or perfectly painted. The eye will blend a reddish bit of background into the red stitching but it will see the startling white canvas.

Keep your tacks closer together to maintain an even tension on your work.

You should cover the edges of your canvas before stitching, it keeps the threads from snagging. A popular way to do this is to use tape. But don't use masking tape — it isn't sticky enough and it degrades. Go to an art supply store (or your LNS) and get Artist's Tape, often called "That White Tape."

Artist's Tape will degrade if exposed to sunlight when on the roll. Keep it in a dark place.

If you forget to tape the canvas before you put it on stretcher bars, don't fret. You can tape the edges of the canvas onto the sides of the stretcher bars. If your tape is wide enough, this could also cover the tacks, which will prevent catching there as well.

Before you tack your needlepoint to stretcher bars, be sure they are square. You can do this by checking with a carpenter's square, checking against a countertop or checking with the corners of a piece of cardboard.

You can make your canvas really tight by using a canvas puller to stretch the canvas gently. This is a tool, sort of like pliers, which artists use to mount their own canvas.

If you are using Evertite stetcher bars, do not put tacks in the corners.

Certain techniques, such as pulled canvas, require tighter canvas than others. Keep this in mind when attaching canvas to frames.

PROJECT IDEAS

Here's an acronym to describe the stitcher's dilemma: **SABLE** *or* **S***tash* **A***ccumulation* **B***eyond* **L***ife* **E***xpectancy. Doesn't that just describe us all? Even so, events come up, new needlepoint designs come out, and sometimes we just want to stitch something new.*

And who knows, those pieces in your stash might just be waiting to become your next project.

Multiple borders can be the focal point of a needlepoint design. Depending on the colors, motifs, and spacing, they can look like Scandinavian knitting, Provençal prints, or exotic fabrics.

Add a transparent layer of color (or shimmer) to your canvas by basting on a layer of chiffon, voile or organdy to the back of the canvas. Baste beyond the edges of the completed area. The stitching and borders will hold the fabric in place.

Why not challenge yourself when you have half-done pieces in your stash? Make it a priority to finish that piece you love but haven't completed. Then treat yourself with something new when it is done.

Here's a nice idea for a present for someone getting married – make a ring bearer pillow. To turn any pillow into a ring bearer pillow, just put a long ribbon in the center of the pillow AFTER you have stitched it, but before the pillow is finished. Knot it once. On the day of the wedding, the ribbon should be knotted again and then used. After the wedding, untie the knots and remove the ribbon.

If you are like me, you probably have bunches of ends and pieces of overdyed thread. Not really enough for anything substantial. Or perhaps you were using two strands of Watercolours for a project and have bunches of single strands. Here's a great way to use them up: combine them with a solid-colored thread in a design. This will give you a subtle, tweeded effect.

Planning a needlepoint from an old piece? Don't count stitches as often some are missing. Trace the outlines and stitch from that. This works unless you are doing a reproduction, then it should be stitch for stitch as the original (mistakes and all).

From Joyce Fletcher via the ANG discussion list: She has been making quite a series of Christmas stockings and is going to do an original design. She writes, "I'll stencil a number of Christmas ornament shapes (not just round balls) and make the background out of long stitches and Charleston threads to simulate the tree. Plus, I'll use up whatever overdyed floss and Medici I have in my stash. After all, God made Christmas trees with lots of textures and shades of green. The Christmas ornaments I will probably make of a variety of stitches, that will make up fast." I just love this idea and wish I needed to make a stocking.

Do you have a hurry up and wait life? I do, so I always have a few small projects to take along with me, even while I wait to pick up the kids after school.

If you have a piece which is slightly smaller than the area for your frame, say the stitching is 4x6 and the frame is 5x7, then add some stitching. For one piece I added a very simple border of three rows of Gobelin Stitches. It was simple, added the right amount, and the gold and peach in the border really sets off the night sky.

Having a scrap bag project, which uses up bits and pieces of thread and unifies it with a common outline, is a great way to use up your stash or to try new threads. Outlining makes a great car project. It fits all the best criteria. The work is easy, in one color only and doesn't require either a chart or much thought. While riding in the car this afternoon I got about ten blocks outlined, so I have a nice big chunk to fill in (the fun part) tonight.

I have a little basket on my desk with some threads in it. Originally they were colors picked as a reference, out of my usual range of colors. To that I added some new threads I just loved. They are there and inspiring new projects.

If I put the little bit of leftover thread away, it may not surface for months, so now I have a little basket (bought at Goodwill for a quarter) where I put the threads for Scrap Bag Needlepoint™. As I work on projects, the potential scraps (single strands of Watercolours, thread samples, the end of a card of Rainbow Gallery thread, etc.) go into the basket. When it is very full, I know it is time to start a new project. Some are pillows (I'm working on the third of these now), some are ornaments, but the fun is learning about new threads and seeing order emerge from the chaos of colors and textures.

Do you have lots of threads of a single color? Why not make a monochrome stitch sampler. Get a piece of canvas and mark random blocks on it. Gather your threads together and get out your stitch dictionary. Pick a thread, a new stitch, and a block. Stitch it. Be sure to make some notes about the stitch. But the end result can be a great piece as well as a wonderful learning experience.

At sales and auctions, look for inexpensive beginner's projects and give them to friends who want to learn to needlepoint.

When your LNS has sales, look for quick projects.

If you can find some old projects (even kits) at your local thrift shop, buy them. There is no rule that says you must stitch them with the included threads.

STITCHES

Stitches are the words in the language of needlepoint. There are hundreds, and they can be varied in so many ways.

Stitches are generally divided into families. Understanding the type of stitch you are using and how it is constructed is an enormous help in choosing stitches and in making your finished pieces look integrated.

Learning about stitches is endlessly fascinating. The more you know, the better you can choose the perfect background for that round vase with flowers, or the right stitch to show off a subtly shaded background.

Even the most experienced stitchers find that they may try several ideas before finding the right stitch. The right stitch keeps the overall project in balance, and makes the composition harmonious. The wrong stitch is uncomfortable to view, and often uncomfortable to stitch. It may not cover the canvas well. It may be difficult to compensate.

Basketweave forms the basis of all diagonal stitches.

Many stitches leave open spaces between units. Vary these stitches by adding other stitches between the units. Cross Stitches, Tent Stitches and Straight Stitches all work really well for this.

Another name for Backstitch, rarely used, is Point de Sable.

Stitches can look completely different if stitched in the opposite direction. For example, a horizontal version of Split Stitch makes a great sky, but the more usual vertical version would look odd.

Stitch Burden Stitch in two colors to give the effect of small scales.

If you are using two threads close to each other in color or value, change the direction or texture of the stitches to make more of a contrast between them.

Tension is a hard aspect of needlepoint to master, but it is an important one. Uneven tension in Basketweave, for example, will result in stitches with slightly different slants. In addition, in any kind of Tent Stitch, hard stitching with different kinds of rows results in different slants, at best, and visible ridges in the front of the needlepoint, at worst.

Do you want to make a stitch which goes over more than one intersection in a metallic thread? Think about using a metallic ribbon for this. Kreinik makes 1/16" and 1/8" ribbons in most of the same colors as their metallic braid. When used for longer stitches, the ribbons give a lovely, smooth finish which is quite unusual.

Great texture can be achieved on a piece by taking a stitch like Scotch and breaking it out of even rows, in other words, offsetting the stitch.

To cover a miter, make one diagonal stitch from inside to outside after the miter is complete.

Overly loose stitches look lumpy, overly tight stitches distort the canvas around them.

Adding French Knots to a piece? Vary the texture by making knots of different sizes (bigger needles, more wraps) and different threads of similar colors. I did this for a beer head, and it looked fantastic.

Compensating by reduction creates a mounded effect. This is because objects get smaller as they get farther away from the eye. So by reducing the size, it looks as if the edges of the object are farther away.

Backstitches made to be wrapped work best if they go over 2 or 3 threads. Longer stitches won't create as nice a line unless they are wrapped with a heavy thread.

Are you outlining using Whipped Backstitch? Stitch one area at a time and wrap it immediately. Often if you are outlining with the same color of thread as the interior of the area, the Backstitches will disappear if you wait to finish the stitch.

Are you stitching an area in Knitting Stitch? Make a reminder for yourself by stitching a line along the edge of the canvas showing the direction of the stitch.

In order to be stable, Backstitches on canvas, as well as Straight Stitches, need to go over at least two threads on the canvas.

Stitches can be grouped into families based on the direction of the stitch (e.g. diagonal), the shape of the stitch (e.g. box), the method in which they are made (e.g. tied) or their use (e.g. accent). Since all stitches in a family share characteristics, look in the same family first when looking to substitute a stitch.

Have you ever wondered if this stitch fits? Except for accent stitches which are meant to be single, three repeats of a stitch should fit into the area in all directions, horizontal, vertical and diagonal.

If there is not enough space for three repeats, the eye will not see a pattern, but only confused stitching.

STITCHING

There are so many little, good ideas which can make your stitching better. And better stitching makes better finished projects.

If you've been stitching for a long time, many of these tips you probably already use, often without thinking about it. Because you're experienced, your hands "know" what to do. But adding the tips which are new to you will improve your stitching.

If you're new to stitching, learning how to stitch better will make the fastest improvement in the quality of the work. I always find it surprising how something little, like counting threads, can suddenly make a stitch make sense.

The smaller the canvas mesh, the shorter your stitching length of thread should be.

Do you have fuzzies left over after you've cut out some stitching? Wrap some masking tape, sticky side out around your hand and pass it over the piece.

Count threads, not holes, as sometimes more than one stitch shares a hole.

If your loops of thread are too loose on the back, the stitches before and after the traveling thread will have a tendency to get loose after the piece is finished and in use.

Neat backs do make a difference. Random tails and long lengths of thread going from area to area can bleed through to the front of the canvas, marring the work.

Do you keep track of how many stitches you do in an area? I'm doing this for a commission (I'm getting paid by the stitch) and I am astonished at how quickly the number of stitches mounts. In an area I stitched last night, I thought maybe there were 200 stitches; there end up being just over 400.

Try it some time for your own edification; you'll be surprised at how much you accomplish.

If you are using Straight Stitches, think about buying Penelope canvas (double thread). The canvas threads are thinner and are less likely to show through.

I just had to rip out a whole bunch of stitches. I stitch tightly and so unstitching is not a possibility; I had to cut everything out. I have one of those little blades to cut the stitches. Here are some tips for doing this.

Assemble your tools (cutter, tweezers, ort container) before you start.

If the area is large, work on it in bits and pieces, not all at once.

Cut the stitching beginning at the edges of the area.

Cut stitches on both the front and back (this makes them easier to pull out).

Use thin slant-ended tweezers to pull the threads.

Watch TV or listen to music while you do this.

Add some extra detail by Backstitching over the finished Tent Stitch. This is great for letters and numbers.

If a few stitches are tighter than the rest, slip a needle underneath them and fluff them a bit.

If you have single stitch eyes in a piece, use a dull metallic for them, it gives the sparkle of real eyes.

Stitching your needlepoint in the correct order can make your pieces look nicer and make them be more enjoyable to stitch.

1. Look at all the threads you have selected and arrange them from lightest to darkest.

2. Pull out of the lineup any fuzzy or furry threads – these will be stitched last.

3. Pull out of the lineup any threads to be used for overstitching, French Knots, or couching. These will be done just before the furry threads.

4. Pull out your background thread. You might want to stitch bits of background all along (I do) or stitch it all at once. But it too goes in a separate pile.

5. Arrange the remaining threads from lightest to darkest. This is the order you should use for stitching.

6. Now find the spots on your canvas where the lightest thread is used. Stitch these.

7. If using Basketweave, stitch from upper right to lower left, slanting in the same direction.

8. For other stitches, follow the correct stitching order for that stitch.

9. As you finish each color, move on to the next color.

10. Start and finish threads with waste knots or by burying the ends in the same color area.

11. Don't carry your thread across more than five threads to another area of the same color. Stop and start the thread.

12. Once all the other stitching is finished, stitch with the furry threads.

13. Brush any areas which need it.

14. Now do the knots, couching and overstitching. Add buttons, cat's whiskers, beading and other final embellishments.

Stitching the background as you go is one way to keep it from seeming endless.

I worked on my Elizabeth Bradley piece while in the Southwest – with all that driving I got lots done. If you are doing something large, like a rug, and want minimal distortion, think about using Victorian Cross Stitch. I'm working the Bradley piece in hand and the piece is very straight. This will make life much easier.

If stitching with light-colored delicate threads, stitch the areas away from your body first and work towards you. This puts less wear on the threads and will keep them cleaner.

Stitching in Basketweave with overdyed thread makes diagonal stripes. To avoid this, either use Continental or stitch in little clumps.

Use a piece of cardboard to cover areas you don't want brushed when you are brushing.

Do you stitch in hand? Start at the center of the canvas and work out; this will keep the stitching neater, since it won't be crumpled as much.

If you will be using a magnifier, stitch the first few stitches without magnification to set a scale for your work.

Are you a lefty? You might find Basketweave easier if you start from the lower left corner and work up.

Going from light colors to dark is critical for wool threads and somewhat less important for cotton threads.

Add texture, not color, to a background by using Pattern Darning and two strands of floss in a color to match the canvas color.

When setting a diagonal pattern in a space, begin in the middle of the longest distance, this will center your pattern.

Do not pull the couching thread tightly when tying the couched thread down; there should be no puckers. The couching thread should lay just on top of the couched thread.

Tying stitches can exit and enter the canvas in the same hole or in different holes, the choice depends on the shape of the couched line, where it sits on the canvas, and your stitching style.

Always make sure the threads you are using for padding are rounded and similar in color to the decorative top thread (so they don't peek through). Pearl cotton is my favorite (this gives the most height).

When I work a Scrap Bag Needlepoint™ design, I keep an extra plastic bag for the ends of threads I've already used. This allows me to use them again (if I like) in a different quadrant, but it also prevents me from pulling them out again and again.

Use two needles to couch, one for the couched thread, and one for the couching thread.

When laying down the couched thread, leave it a little loose on the face of the canvas and do not unthread, or tie off the couched thread on the back until it is couched down. This allows you to adjust the tension and draw up slack.

To avoid those annoying little twists ribbon threads get at the ends of stitches, use a bigger needle first to enlarge the holes slightly.

If you are working on a project where you have several areas in different colors in a similarly sized box stitch, then you need to think about how the areas will line up with each other. An incredibly neat way to do this is to have them line up exactly. Begin by stitching one of the areas with a box stitch, then use one of these box stitches to place the first box stitch in a different area. You can't always do this, but when you can, it's a nice little flourish.

Need to remember where you need to stitch while finding your place in a book and threading your needle? Use a beaded stitch counter.

Always couch in the same direction as you laid down the couched thread. Begin where the needle emerged from the canvas and end where it came back into the canvas. This has smoother results and lets you adjust the tension of the couched thread.

Stitch any areas which are "behind" the couching completely before beginning to couch. This keeps bits of painted canvas from sticking out around the couched line.

You can get an interesting effect for a small spot by thickening the stitch. Start with a thin thread, make a Straight Stitch and go over it again and again until you are happy with how raised it is.

It's basic but bears repeating — go up in a clean hole and down in a dirty hole. This keeps the stitching neat.

Even if you think you can't, you can make variations of stitches. One easy way to do this is to frame units of the stitch, or groups of units, with Tent Stitch.

Another way to vary a stitch is to "explode" it by separating the units from each other by an open thread.

The back of the canvas wears more than the front. Therefore, strive to have good coverage on the back.

Objects which get heavy use should never have stitches which cover more than three intersections.

You can change a stitch's size by changing the number of stitches in a unit, or by increasing or decreasing their length.

Many stitches have layers (think of Rice Stitch for example); you can easily vary these by using a different thread for each layer.

Techniques

Blackwork, Bargello, Canvas Appliqué, Pulled Canvas – once you get started in needlepoint, there are so many wonderful techniques to explore. Some of them, like Blackwork, have been around for centuries. Others, like Bargello, are so easy they could be a first needlepoint project.

Many of these techniques are specialized enough that if you just stitch any old way, you will be disappointed with the results. A small amount of knowledge will help assure that the results of your stitching are outstanding.

Couching also needs to stand above the fabric, so choose couched threads which are heavier than would be used for stitching.

Threads used for the top layer of padded stitches should be flat. This assures that the top layer will be smooth and without distinct stitches. Ribbons of all types are flat threads. Stranded threads, such as Splendor or floss, can be turned into flat threads by plying and recombining.

If two lines of couching intersect; do not make ties at the intersecting point, make them on either side to secure the couching without piercing the other line.

Couching can be done at irregular intervals along a line of couched thread. Couching stitches need to be made closer together along curves to make the curve smooth.

Use a laying tool when making padded stitches to keep the threads flat and smooth.

Each layer of padding (and the top decorative layer) should be successively larger. This will give the area rounded, natural edges, instead of being abrupt, more like a hill than a cliff.

Padding stitches do not have to have much thread on the back; it is perfectly acceptable to move to the next hole on the same side of the stitch when making the next stitch. You do not need to go back to the side where you began the previous stitch.

The direction of the stitches for each layer should be perpendicular to the layers above and/or below it. By doing this, each layer will have stitches which do not get lost between the stitches of the other layers.

If you are appliquéing one piece of canvas onto another, make sure you leave a wide margin around the piece which will be appliquéd, this will make it easier to attach. Instead of a needle, use a fine crochet hook. This can come out from under the canvas, hook one of those thread ends ,and easily pull it to the backside of the canvas. And it's much easier than threading and unthreading each canvas thread!

With waste canvas, having generous margins will make it easier to pull out the canvas threads after you have finished stitching.

If you are doing Longstitch, always use a frame; otherwise, the stitches won't lay flat on the canvas.

If you are using Blackwork as a filling, you can make the outlines stand out more by using a raised edge, like Whipped Backstitch, or outlining in beads.

Threads used for Blackwork should be no wider than the width of a canvas thread.

Blackwork diagrams can be confusing to needlepointers. This is because needlepoint stitch diagrams mimic needlepoint canvas with lines often starting and stopping in holes on the grid. Blackwork diagrams are just the opposite, the intersections on the grid are the holes on the canvas.

In Blackwork, center the pattern in every area by beginning in the center of the longest row.

In Blackwork, or any open technique, try to hide your traveling threads by moving from motif to motif along a line which will be covered by stitching.

Another way to hide threads in Blackwork is to use Double Running Stitch, which takes two passes to complete a line.

Stitch the first line of Bargello from the center of the canvas to the edge and then go back and do the second half of the line. This will automatically center the pattern.

When stitching the first line of Bargello, start in the center, leave about half the length of thread as a tail. Then you have it right there to finish the line.

Always stitch Bargello so that the path of the thread on the **back** of the canvas is the longest possible. You may come up in a dirty hole and down in a clean hole, but it's worth it. This creates a fuller back, which will make the front wear better.

Bargello stitches can be hard to secure. Begin Bargello (except the first line) with a Bargello Tuck, named by Jean Hilton. Pass the thread through about one inch of stitches, then, skipping one thread. Return it back through about 1/2 inch. This secures the thread.

Stitch Turkeywork from the bottom of an area to the top. This prevents getting the loops stuck in your stitching.

Make the loops in Turkeywork slightly longer than the finished length. It's better to begin too long than too short.

Using very sharp, pointed scissors for trimming Turkeywork will make the job easier.

Don't cut Turkeywork loops until the area is completely stitched. Then cut everything. Then, and only then, trim. Trim a little bit at a time and measure the untrimmed area with a trimmed area, just like getting your hair cut. Doing this will allow you to control the ends, which are fuzzy while you stitch, and control the length of the trimmed Turkeywork.

Almost all stitches can become pulled stitches. Just pull in the opposite direction of the stitch after every stitch. The effect can be quite striking and completely different from the non-pulled version of the stitch.

Only use strong, unstranded threads for pulled canvas. Linen and pearl cotton are perfect.

If you want the maximum effect for the open areas in pulled canvas, use a thread which matches the canvas color.

If you want the stitches to be accented, use a color which contrasts with the canvas color.

Always remember that in pulled canvas, the canvas color is a factor in the design, and choose accordingly.

Don't want to stitch that background? Before you begin to stitch, think about painting the canvas. Mask off the design, so you won't paint it and then sponge paint, brush or stencil a background. This looks best when more than one color is used to create a background of real depth.

Threads used for darning patterns should be flat and about the width of the holes in the canvas.

Don't start a row of Pattern Darning unless you have plenty of thread to complete it.

In Pattern Darning never move from row to row inside the stitching area, this distorts the threads. Move the thread either on the back through the stitches of another area or with a tiny running stitch outside the edge of the stitching.

Pattern Darning is my absolute favorite effect for skies. It can cover the canvas densely, but it is lower and therefore lighter, than Tent Stitch. To get some of the variation present in real skies, I choose hand-dyed, semisolid or slightly variegated shades of blue or blue-gray.

You can easily convert a Filet Crochet chart to needlepoint. The solid areas are Mosaic Stitch. The open areas are open squares with Straight Stitches over two threads on each side.

Filet Crochet patterns are particularly effective as needlepoint when done on dark canvas.

The lacy effect which happens when using a subtly overdyed cream thread is great for stitching filet crochet patterns.

Shadow Stitching is a technique which uses thinner threads and open stitches to allow a beautifully painted canvas to show. But, if you Shadow Stitch in all one color, it may look as if the canvas is washed out.
Try retaining the stitch pattern but changing the color of the thread to match the canvas.

Shadow Stitching makes for tremendous backgrounds. Because the threads used are so thin, it always looks lighter than the focal point of the canvas.

Try using very thin metallics, such as Treasure Braid Petite or Kreinik Very Fine (#4) braid, for Shadow Stitching. Pick a color which matches the area's color. It adds shimmer, but not color.

THREADS

Threads, threads, threads! Not only are they the basic material of needleart, they are, for me at least, the stuff dreams are made of. When I go into a needlework store, I am more entranced by the threads than by the canvases. Seeing the chance combination of threads on my desk inspires projects. Seeing a painted canvas makes me think first about what threads to use, and, only then, what stitches will bring it to life.

Way back (in the '70s and '80s) the emphasis was on using similar threads throughout a canvas. You didn't mix wool with silk, or do a portion of the canvas in pearl cotton. But today anything goes. We have so many different threads to use, so many different textures and so many colors, that anything goes.

One way to make Fuzzy Stuff (from Rainbow Gallery) more fuzzy is to go **up** in a dirty hole and **down** in a clean hole – the opposite of what you normally would do.

Hate using Fray-Check™ for metallic threads, but need to stop the raveling? Use an acid-free glue stick. Look in scrapbooking supplies.

Sometimes I have to get fibers over the phone and then I feel like a dummy trying to describe the color. DMC color cards are widely available. If you have one and the shop has one, you can use that as a baseline for describing the color you want. It makes it that much easier to get a match.

Many threads have labels which can't be kept, or are twisted such that they must be opened before cutting. To keep the threads in some sort of order after doing this, I put them onto hangtags with big holes cut in them. Many companies make these, but you can also make your own by buying a BIG hole punch and manila hangtags.

Metallic threads dull scissors, so keep a pair of them just for cutting metallics.

Cut pearl cotton easily and get perfect stitching lengths by cutting the skein, with the labels still on, at the bottom twist of the skein (where there is only the twist).

If you are not sure how many strands of a thread to use, stitch a few stitches on the margins of the canvas to check. Does the canvas show? The thread is too thin. If the holes around the stitch are distorted, then it's probably too thick.

It's always a good idea (which I don't always follow) to buy enough of a color to finish a project. Some manufacturers are more reliable than others, but ALL threads can have changes in dye lots. This is because of the nature of dyeing. This is especially important for backgrounds and for threads used in large areas of color.

There are translucent organdy ribbons on the market made for stitching. Depending on the size of ribbon, the stitch, and the number of times you go over the stitch you can get effects from almost transparent to intense colors.

Tired of putting together floss and blending filament? Try Hi-Lites from Rainbow Gallery – it gives the same effect in one thread.

Want to cut ideal stitching lengths ahead of time? Buy an 18" ruler and wrap the thread around it. Cut it at both ends and knot the bundle. You have perfect 18" stitching lengths without guessing every time.

Keep those odds and ends of thread handy; you will find that many of them are just perfect for accents.

Are you overwhelmed with threads you'll never use? Make tassels, or give them to a knitting friend to make fringe.

Some threads (especially linens) have two numbers associated with them, like 10/5. The first number indicates the diameter of the ply and the second the number of plies. With diameter, the lower the number the thicker the ply.

Do your own thread of the month club – pick a color and buy a new thread that color each month. At the end of the year use them to do a project.

Knitters test yarn by making a swatch. Have you thought of testing a color or thread by making a test swatch of the stitch you will be using? You'll learn from this. Perhaps with an overdyed you will see new colors emerge. You might find that the stitch doesn't cover well, or that the scale is wrong. And if you save and label your samples, you will start to make your own stitch and thread reference.

Wishing you had some color cards for your stash? Make your own. Buy multi-pocket page protectors, like the ones for slides. Clip a bit of thread and attach it to a small card with the thread information on the back. Now you have a reference for the future.

Cotton threads come in different lengths of fiber, called staples. The longer the staple, the better the yarn for needlepoint.

Mercerization is the process which makes cotton floss and pearl shiny. Unmercerized cotton is matte.

If your thread is packaged in pull-out skeins, or wound on spools or cards, always thread the oldest cut end. Then you will be stitching with the nap of the thread. If you don't know which end is oldest, rub the thread under your nose or against your cheek, and find out which way is smoother, this is the nap of the thread. Thread the top.

Do you need a stiff thread which matches the color of the canvas? Why not unravel a thread of needlepoint canvas for an interesting effect? Since the lengths might be short, you may want to unravel threads from longer pieces in your stash.

Using a laying tool when working with stranded threads (like floss) or ribbon threads (like Neon Rays) helps keep the threads from twisting and makes the stitches look better.

Very thin metallics, especially in white or black, can give the illusion of lace on canvas.

From my friend Michelle of Come to the Point!: Increase your stash of Watercolours easily. Find a list in alphabetical order and check off the colors you have. Then, once a month, buy 5 skeins, buying in alphabetical order, starting with "A." This will give you some wonderful variety. The same can be done with any thread with easily found color names.

I am working on a piece which uses lots of RibbonFloss® and I've got it on a spool, so it comes off the spool in nice corkscrew curls. Straightening it makes things much easier and I do this by running it between a fingernail and fingertip.

This doesn't always work, however. Why? Because it needs to be done with the fingernail on the outside of the curl. Do it on the inside and it doesn't work. This is also why curly ribbon sometimes doesn't curl but straightens instead.

So make straight outside, make curly inside.

Why it took almost 35 years of doing needlepoint to figure this out, I'll never know.

Some threads are a bit flyaway and the tails don't hold together, so the needle comes unthreaded. Try putting clear nail polish on the end and let it dry before stitching.

Inevitably there will be times when you run out of a thread and end up needing to substitute. When this happens, think carefully about the characteristics of the thread you have used to find something which will work with your piece. Threads have two major characteristics, color and texture. Pick the one which is more important in the piece and look for the closest match in that aspect first. So, because the texture was what was really important in this ornament, I am using a close, but not exact match in Fiesta, for Lystwist, a discontinued thread.

You turn a stranded round thread (like floss) into a flat thread by separating the plies and reassembling the strand.

Do you want a shimmering look to your stitching? Try adding blending filament, Treasure Braid Petite, or other thin metallic to your stitching bundle.

Recently I was working on a piece with a primitive bird on it, and wanted it to be a real focal point. It's a red cardinal and rather blocky, so I used Shadow-Dyed Spring II from Needle Necessities in bright red in a giant Scotch Stitch. And what a delightful surprise! Because of the shadow-dyed effect, and the unusual texture of the thread – it looks like crushed velvet. The effect is quite elegant and is something you should try on your Christmas ornaments. I am now busily thinking up other pieces to use this great thread.

Separating threads and recombining them is important for smooth needlepoint. Pulling straight out from the thread bundle keeps knots from forming. But did you know that you can tell if you are separating with or against the grain of the thread right after you pull out the first strand?

If the remaining thread hangs down straight from your hand, you have pulled with the grain. If it has bunched up, you have pulled against the grain. Reverse the pulled thread and grab the other end of the remaining threads before separating the next strand.

If your chosen thread is just a bit too thin to cover your canvas, don't give up and choose another thread! If the canvas is painted, the thin coverage may not show (especially if the painting is the same color). But if the canvas is not painted, you can add a strand or so of thread to your main thread to add unnoticeable thickness.

The key is to choose the right thread to add. If you want to add a bit of shimmer, use a metallic – Kreinik #4, Treasure Braid Petite, Sparkle Braid, or blending filament. If it is a wool or furry thread use a strand of crewel wool. Lorikeet from Gloriana is my favorite for this because it is a bit thinner and smoother than Appleton. For smooth threads, use a strand or two of floss.

In any case, match your added thread to the main thread's color as closely as possible.

You'll be surprised at how well this works!

Never do Double Running Stitch with overdyes, it makes dotted lines.

Silk & Ivory has several colors which make outstanding backgrounds. These colors are very pale and work with many kinds of canvases. This was brought home to me tonight as I was at my stitching group. One of my friends was working on a Jean Smith canvas which had lovely flowers of many different colors. The color for the background had been under discussion for several weeks as we stitched. Almost every color of the rainbow is somewhere in the canvas so every color we thought of we discarded.

It's pedal to the metal time and she had to decide this week. We settled upon the palest green shade of Silk & Ivory, Cucumber. And it looks great! This color and ones like it (Pail Gray, Crab, Blue Yonder, Pink Lemonade, Sand, and Candlelight) all read pretty much as "white" but they add a subtle wash of color which is very attractive.

Consider them for your next background. They are some of my favorites!

Don't double threads in order to have two stitching strands. This makes a thread which doesn't cover quite as well.

When you are test driving a thread, be sure to use it several ways. I always try to make a small block (usually 1/2 inch) of Basketweave as well as a block of a decorative stitch. The Basketweave will give you a base for exploring the thread and tell you something about its coverage. It will also tell you if the color is solid enough to work in diagonal rows. The decorative stitch will tell you how well this thread works as an accent.

For many threads, a stitching length longer than 18" starts to show the wear.

Persian wool strands, especially from older skeins, may not be all the same width. In any three-strand bundle there is a small, medium and a large thread. To get even stitching widths when using Persian wool, bundle a small and a large or two mediums.

Keeping the tags with your threads after you begin using them can help you match color numbers, manufacturers and dye lots.

From a reader: To get rid of twists in threads, hold each end and pull sharply.

If you can't keep the labels with the threads, buy bags you can write on or hangtags for threads and transfer the information from the labels to the tags.

To learn about new threads, buy the colors you use most often and check your stash when starting a canvas. Greens are always a good choice since there are so many greens in nature.

When using a chainette thread, put clear nail polish or Fray-Check™ on the end to stop it from unraveling.

You can reduce raveling on a chainette thread by using a needle one size larger than your usual size.

From a reader: Strip and lay several lengths of floss at once.

From a reader: You can use totally unraveled chainette threads by laying them on the canvas and couching them down for really great texture.

Pearl cotton is slightly thicker when the stitch slants in one direction rather than slanting in the other direction.

You can make fatter French Knots by using more strands of your thread instead of making more wraps.

Dark-colored threads are thinner than light-colored threads. This is because the fiber has more dye which weighs down the thread.

Trebizond silk unravels for left-handed stitchers, but not for right-handed ones because of the direction of the twist.

Fibers, the stuff threads are made of, are classified as three types: protein, vegetable, and synthetic. Protein fibers come from animals and are silk and wool. Vegetable fibers comes from plants and include cotton, linen and hemp. Synthetic fibers are man-made like nylon or polyester. Each fiber has different characteristics and takes dyes in different ways. In fact, you use different dyes on animal and plant fibers.

From a reader: You can slap your skein of floss on your hand to make the end come out more easily.

Are you going to bead a solid area on 18 mesh canvas? Don't use regular (size 11) seed beads) Petite seed beads (size 15) fit better.

From Graceful Lily Needlework, a blackwork designer: If you are using Double Running Stitch, use the shoelace method to stitch. Stitch with the first end until it is about two-third's used, then thread the needle with the other end and continue. This gives you fewer ends to weave in.

If you use two needles with the shoelace method, it goes much faster. You unthread and rethread less often.

Keep your scraps of thread to use as accents. I'm working on a large multi-canvas project and one color is used for fewer than ten stitches in the entire project. This is the perfect place to use some of those scraps.

You can make foliage more lifelike by combining strands of an overdyed green with a solid green and stitching in Continental.

TRAVELING WITH NEEDLEPOINT

I wonder what people who don't do needlework do when they travel. I had a job where I traveled about 80 percent of the time. Having needlepoint to do kept me happy in the evenings in my hotel room, kept me content during the inevitable plane delays, and allowed me to make many lovely things. Now that I mostly travel by car, I find that having a needlepoint project with me always makes the time go faster and my life easier.

A part of traveling with needlepoint is stitching in places which aren't the best environments -- the beach, dimly lit hotel rooms, airports after security has taken away your scissors. Traveling successfully with needlepoint can mean taking these environments into account and planning for them. Once you do, you may find it more fun to stitch on the road than at home.

When you are traveling, pack a 100-watt bulb to replace the bulb in a lamp in your hotel room.

Going on an airplane anytime soon? Prepare stitching kits which will be in anything carried on. I bought a plastic case of gum to hold my traveling supplies. It has in it extra needles, but only a few, blunt scissors and a needle threader. Drop this in my project bag and I'm ready to go.

If the poor light in hotel rooms is a problem for you, put a bright lightbulb in your checked luggage, well wrapped, and replace the hotel bulbs with that. Just remember to bring it home with you!

Going to the beach or pool and want to do some needlepoint? Make sure it is something which is lightweight (this is not the time for the wool pillow) and has colorfast threads (in case it gets wet).

Put into your stitching kit for trips or classes a portable ort container. This could be a mint tin, an origami box, or even a small cardboard jewelry box. Use it during class and then empty it before leaving.

Stuck for an ort container when away from home? Use an empty cup.

Traveling with a floor stand? Disassemble it and use masking tape to tape it together. Put the hardware in a plastic bag.

Never travel with your expensive scissors. Buy an inexpensive pair (Mass Marketers are great for this) and put them with your travel project. Then you won't mind if they get thrown out.

Look for blunt scissors (for kids) or baby nail scissors for travel.

Do you spend lots of time in the car? I keep a small, not too hard, needlepoint project in the car to work on while I wait. They need to be small and on stretcher bars so that they fit with the wheel in the way. They shouldn't have stitches which require pulling or couching. I love Christmas ornaments for this.

If you are going on a beach vacation, think about doing a plastic canvas project; it is far more resistant to water than canvas. 14 mesh plastic canvas uses the same threads as 18 mesh canvas. Since it's easy to finish the projects, you can complete them while there.

From my friend Michelle of Come to the Point!: If you are working on plastic canvas and it starts to get soft because of the heat, put it in the fridge for an hour to stiffen it.

Traveling by car? Work on projects which don't need stands or use large frames. Many people find these uncomfortable (not to say dangerous) in cars.

There is probably nothing in the world worse than the fare in airport bookstores. All your favorite magazines are between issues, there isn't a paperback in sight you want to read, and all the hardbound books are too expensive. It is hours until your flight. Needlepoint can come to the rescue. In my traveling days, I always kept a "plane project" in my briefcase. It had to be small, easily portable, and something I liked but that wasn't urgent to do (this isn't the place for projects with deadlines).

I put the project, any instructions, and the threads and some needles, into a zipper bag and carried it in my bag.

You don't know how many times those little projects have saved me when I finished my other projects and was stuck at an airport.

Lighting in airports and on planes is poor. Pick projects to work on which have easily distinguishable colors.

When traveling by air, bring a self-addressed, stamped padded envelope with you. Anything you can't bring past security and can't live without, you can put in the envelope and send home.

I have added a "car piece" to my rotation system. This is the piece which goes along with me everywhere. The car piece needs to be mostly or completely Basketweave, should be small (so it is easy to carry) and be easy to see.

I like geometrics for my travel projects, the repetitive stitching in many areas makes them easy to stitch when the lighting is poor.

If you are stuck in a plane or an airport for many hours, don't forget to take breaks. Look around every couple of minutes to avoid eyestrain and get up and stretch, or take a little walk every hour or so. This prevents fatigue and is good for you — even if it's only a walk to get more coffee.

About the Cover

The needlepoint pieces on the cover are examples of Janet's stitch guides and original needlepoint. For more information about her stitch guides, products and classes, see her website at http://www.napaneedlepoint.com.

The pieces pictured are:

Front Cover:
Happy Halloween Advent Calendar: Melissa Shirley Designs
> http://www.melissashirleydesigns.com

Happy Spring (detail): Happy Heart Designs
> http://www.happyheartdesigns.com

Cabin: Cat's Cradle Designs
> http://www.catscradleneedlepoint.com

I Love Needlepoint: Cat's Cradle Designs
> http://www.catscradleneedlepoint.com

All designs are copyright their designer and used with permission.

Back Cover:
Mini Socks from Napa Needlepoint:
center: Scrap Bag Needlepoint
sides: Bargello Reinvented

http://www.napaneedlepoint.com

ABOUT THE AUTHOR

Janet M. Perry is one of the leading writers of
needlepoint stitch guides in the world. She
writes innovative guides for needlepoint
canvases from over 20 designers. She puts into
practice her motto to make needlepoint fast, fun
and affordable.

She is an expert in needlepoint, both on the Web
and through her writing as the Needlepoint Pro
for *Cross-Stitch & Needlework* magazine. She
works with deigners, shops, and thread
manufacturers on new products and regularly
reports on trends in needlepoint.

Visit her website
(http://www.napaneedlepoint.com) or blog
(http://www.nuts-about-needlepoint.com) to
learn about her newest products.